all woman

CABARET

© 2007 by International Music Publications Ltd
First published in 2006 by International Music Publications Ltd
International Music Publications Ltd is a Faber Music company
3 Queen Square
London
WC1N 3AU

Arranging and engraving: Artemis Music Ltd (www.artemismusic.com)

Printed in England by Caligraving Ltd
All rights reserved

ISBN10: 0-571-52448-6
EAN13: 978-0-571-52448-8

To buy Faber Music publications or to find out about the full range of titles available,
please contact your local music retailer or Faber Music sales enquiries:
Faber Music Ltd, Burnt Mill, Elizabeth Way, Harlow, CM20 2HX England
Tel: +44 (0) 1279 82 89 82   Tel: +44 (0) 1279 82 89 83
sales@fabermusic.com   fabermusic.com

all woman
CABARET

ALMOST LIKE BEING IN LOVE

Words by Alan Jay Lerner
Music by Frederick Loewe

Moderato ♩ = 60

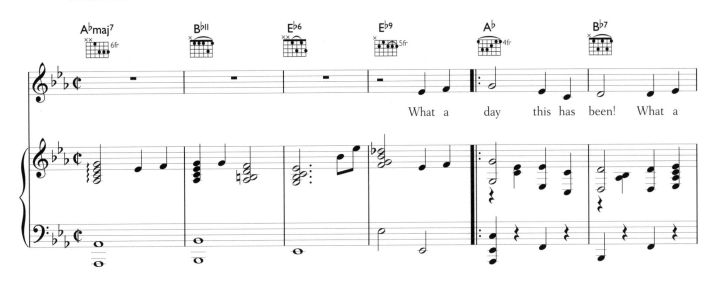

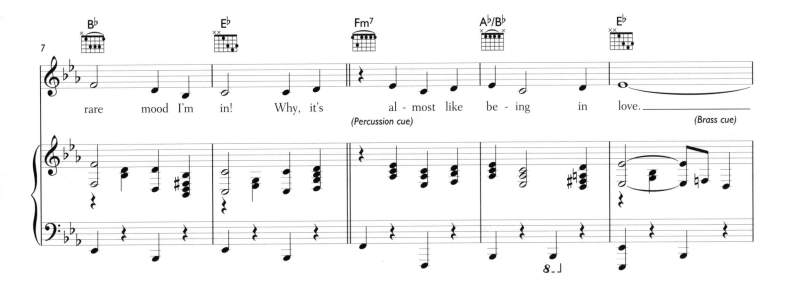

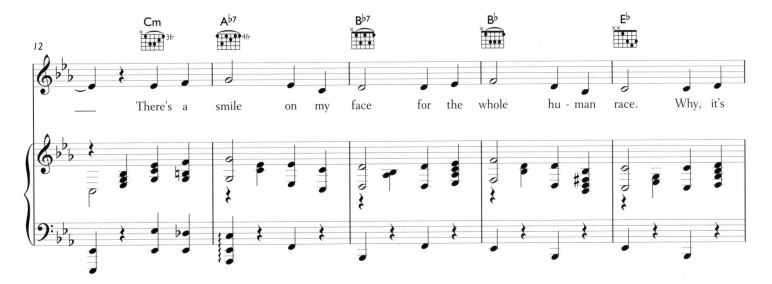

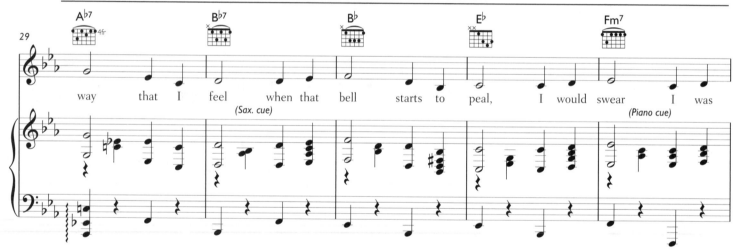

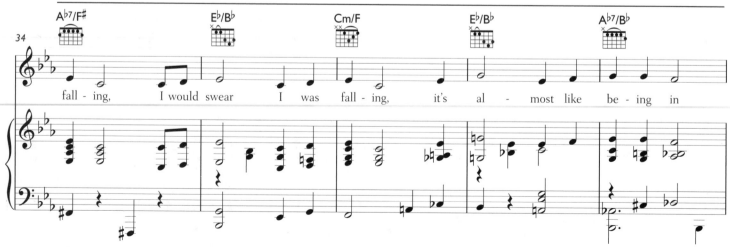

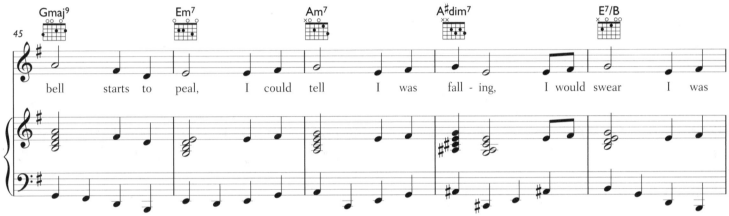

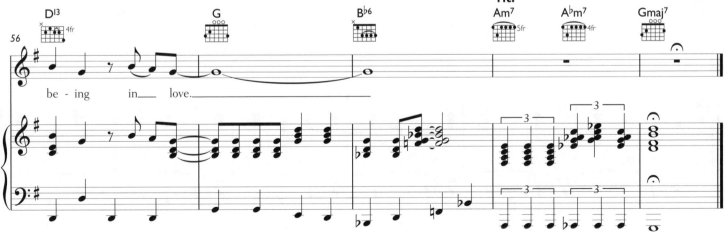

ANOTHER OPENIN', ANOTHER SHOW

Words and Music by Cole Porter

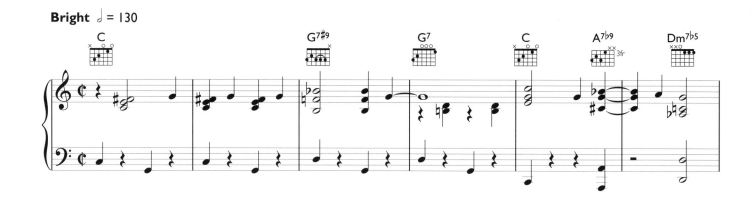

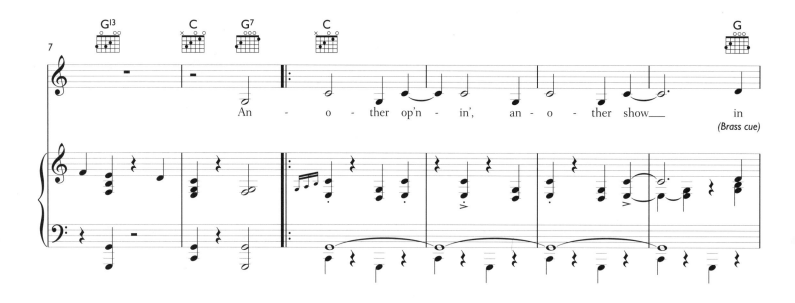

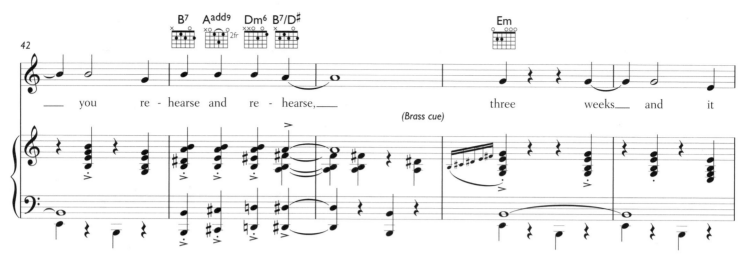

_____ you re-hearse and re-hearse,_____ (Brass cue) three weeks_____ and it

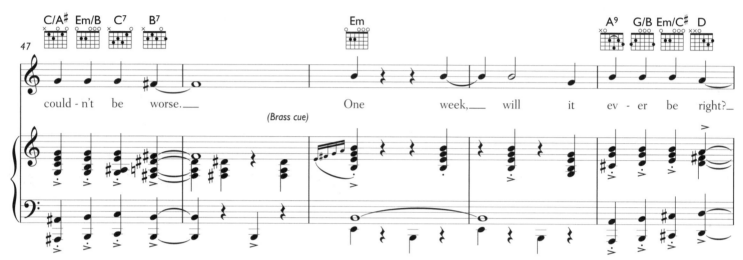

could-n't be worse._____ (Brass cue) One week,_____ will it ev-er be right?

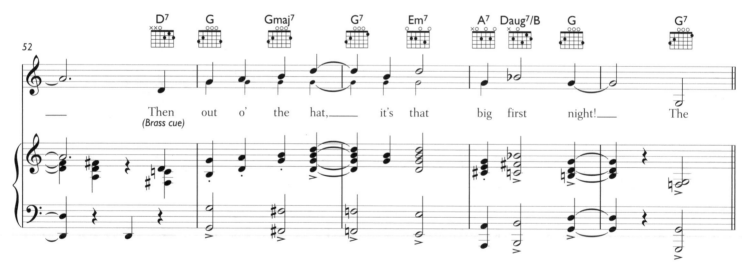

_____ Then out o' the hat,_____ it's that big first night!_____ The
(Brass cue)

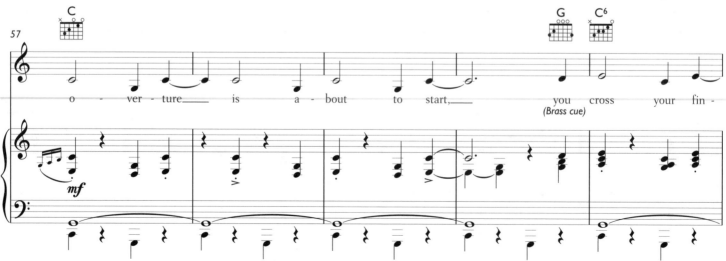

o - ver-ture_____ is a - bout to start,_____ you cross your fin -
(Brass cue)

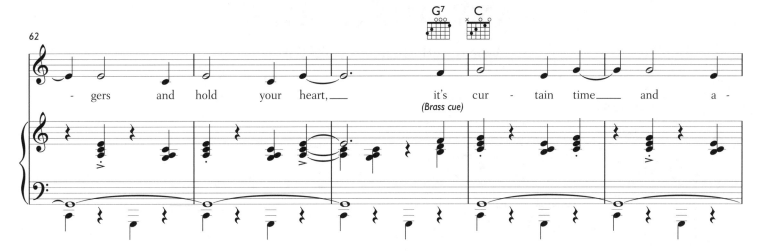

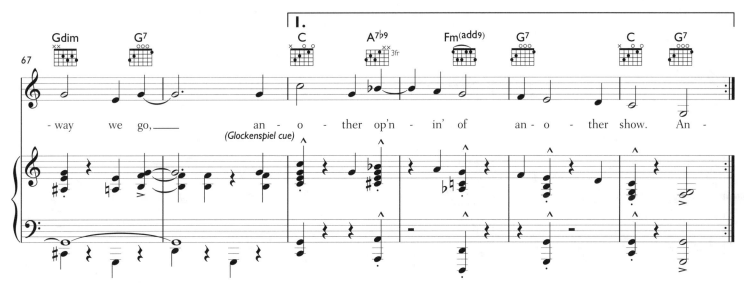

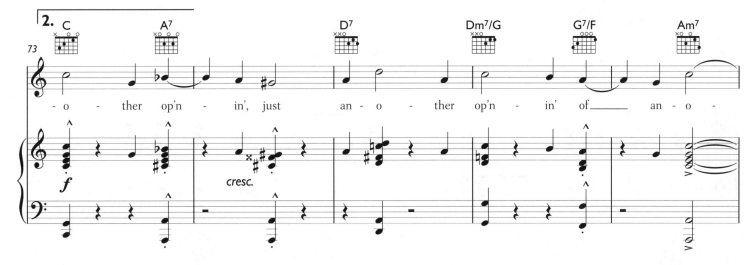

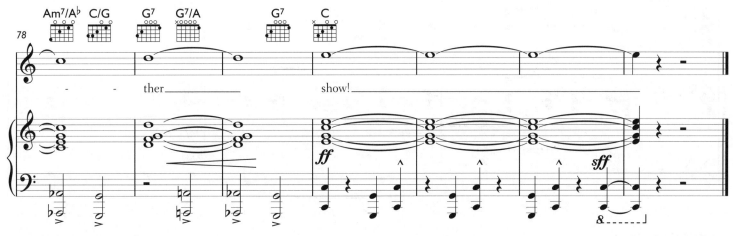

ANYTHING GOES

Words and Music by Cole Porter

THE BEST YEARS OF MY LIFE

Words and Music by Stephen Davis and Will Jennings

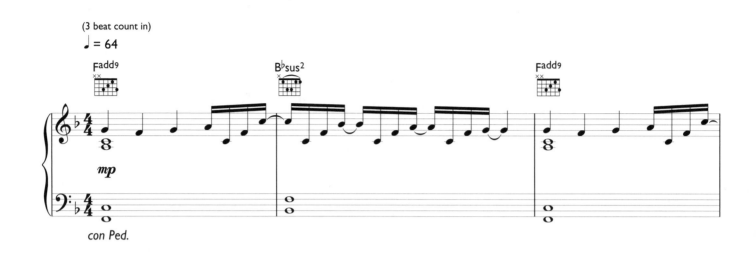

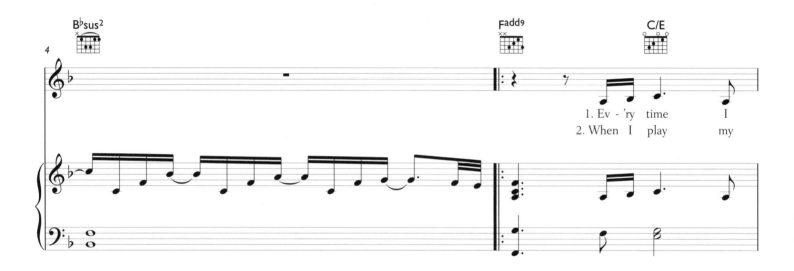

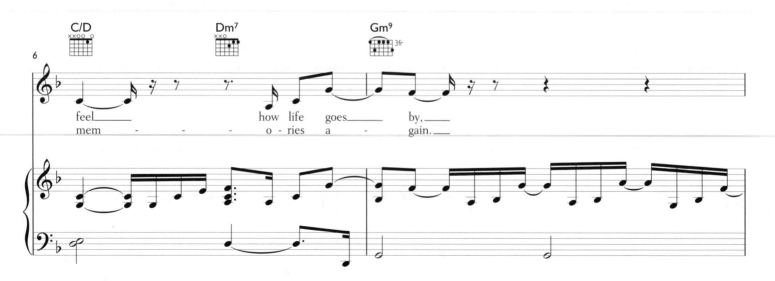

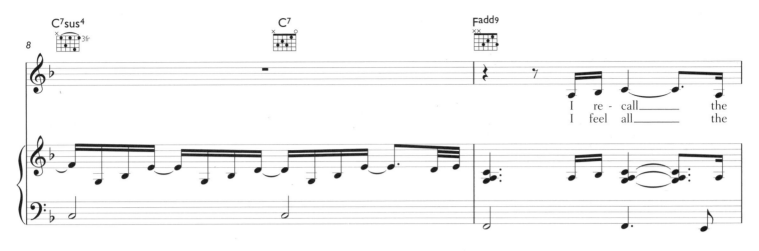

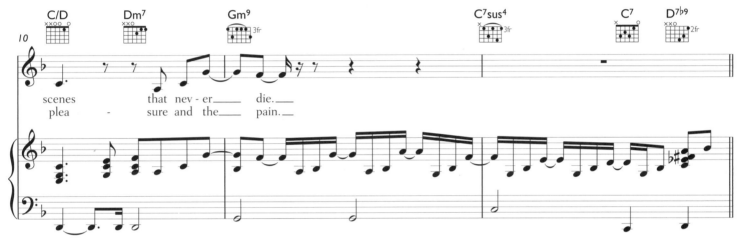

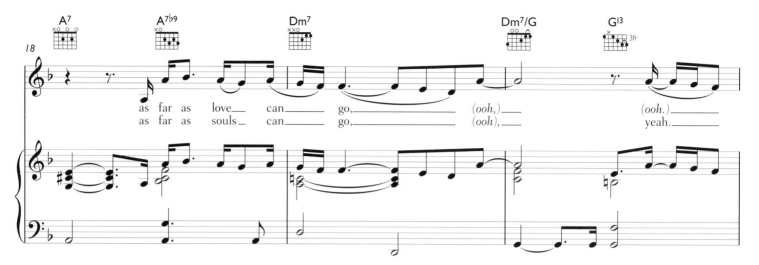

as far as love___ can_____ go,_____ (ooh,)_____ (ooh.)_____
as far as souls___ can____ go,_____ (ooh),___ yeah.____

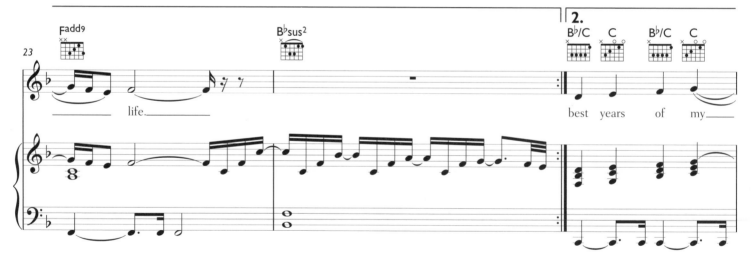

You've___ giv-en me_____ the best years of my____
You've___ giv-en me_____ the

_____ life._____ best years of my___

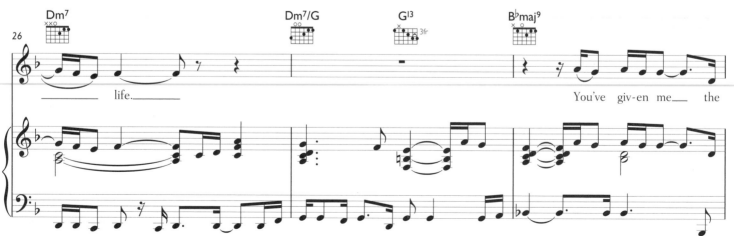

_____ life._____ You've giv-en me___ the

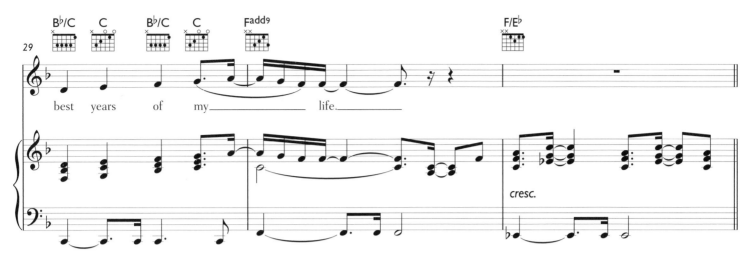

best years of my_____ life._____

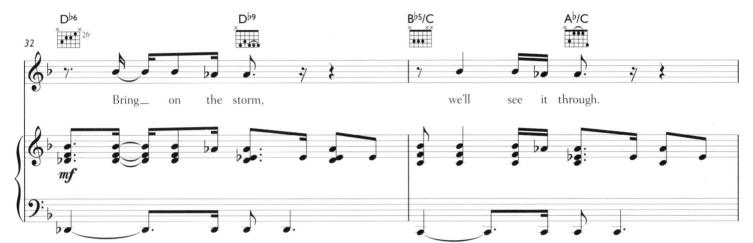

Bring__ on the storm, we'll see it through.

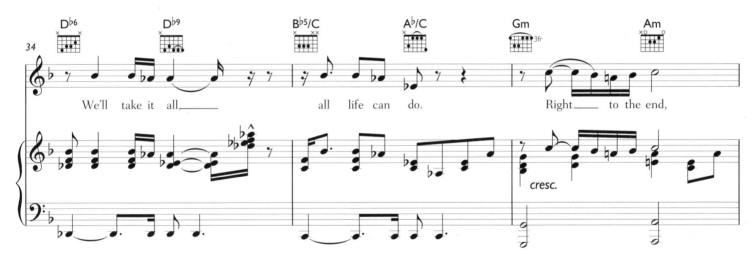

We'll take it all,_____ all life can do. Right____ to the end,

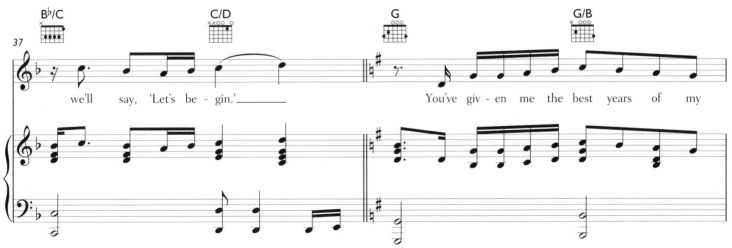

we'll say, 'Let's be - gin.'_____ You've giv - en me the best years of my

FOR ONCE IN MY LIFE

Words by Ronald Miller
Music by Orlando Murden

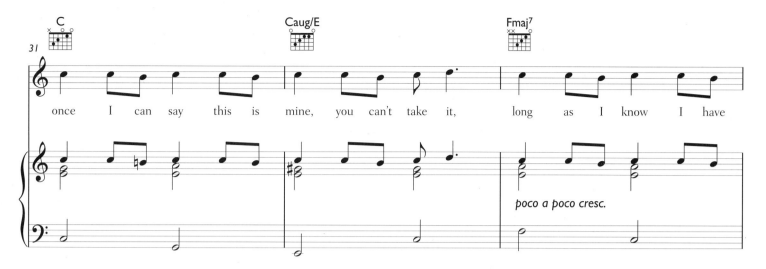

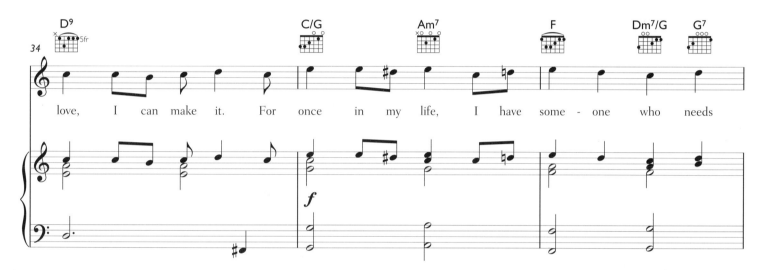

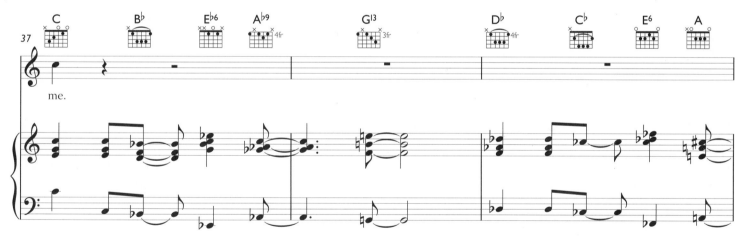

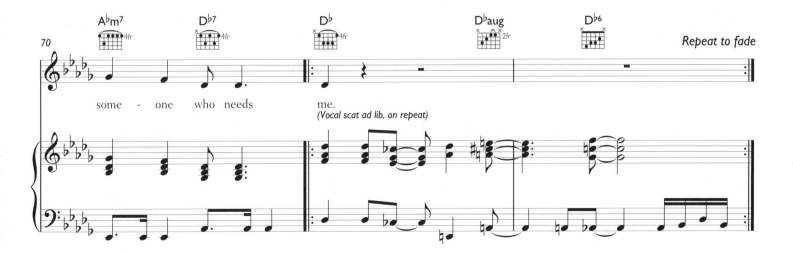

GOLDFINGER

Words by Leslie Bricusse and Anthony Newley
Music by John Barry

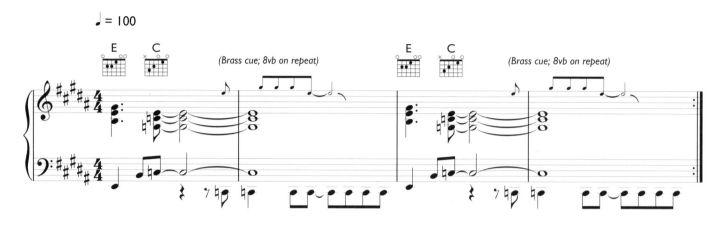

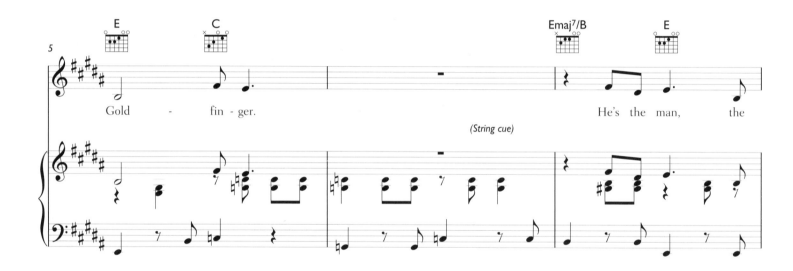

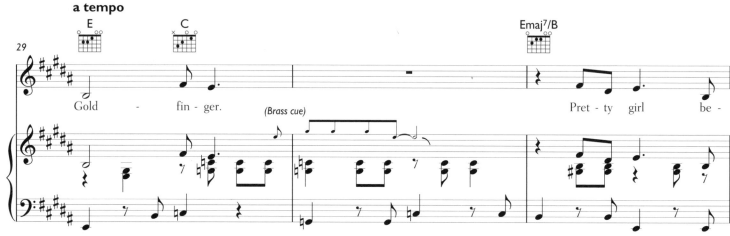

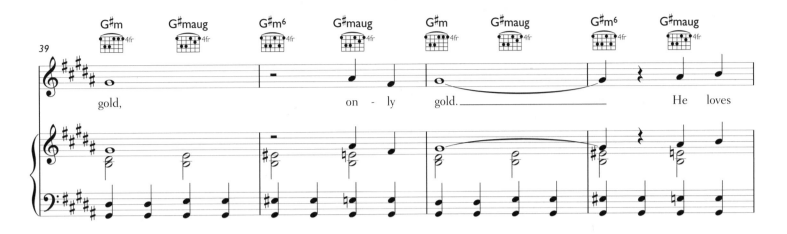

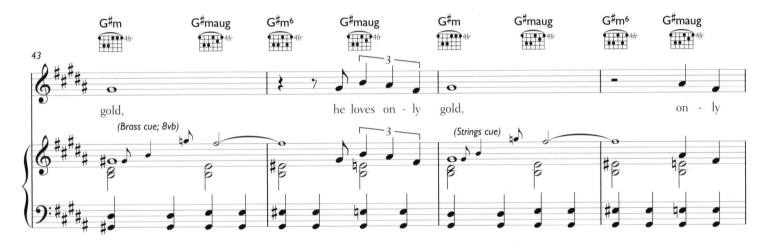

I GOT RHYTHM

Music and Lyrics by George Gershwin and Ira Gershwin

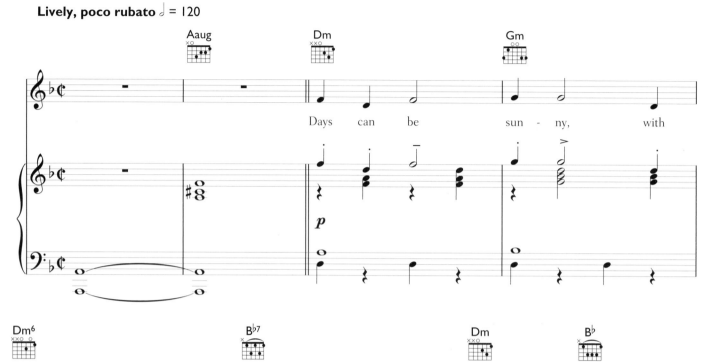

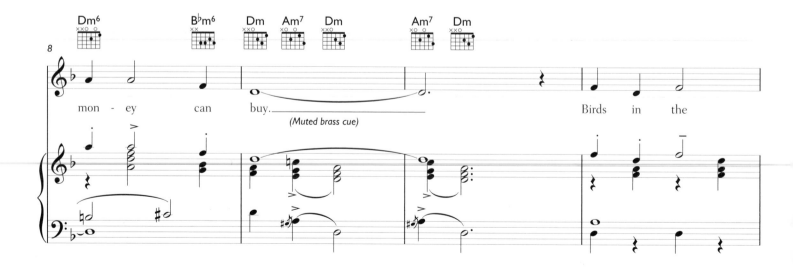

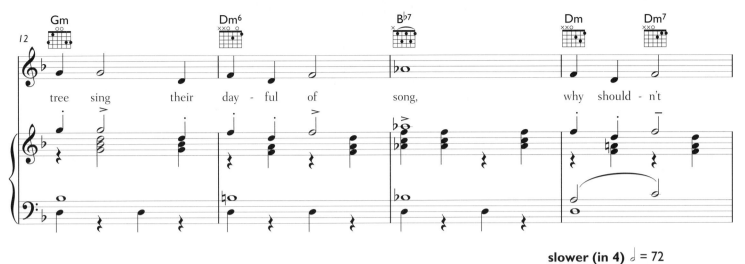

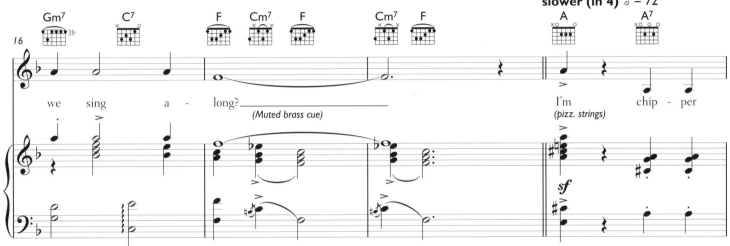

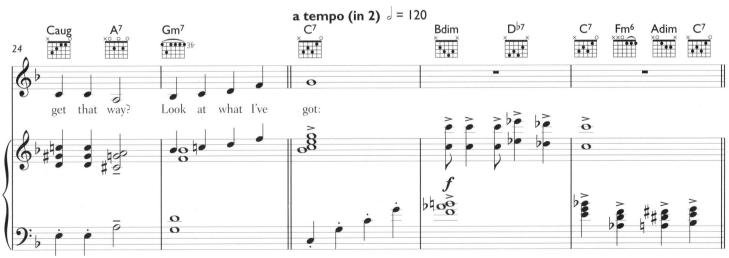

with abandon

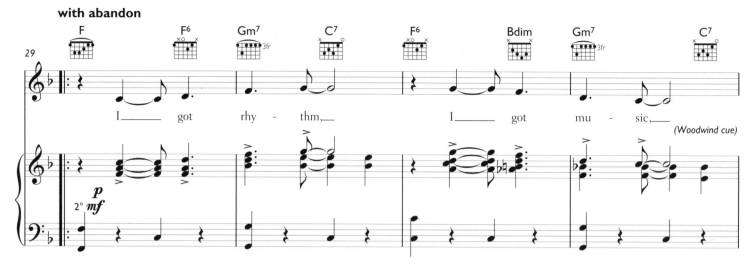

I_____ got rhy - thm,_____ I_____ got mu - sic,_____ *(Woodwind cue)*

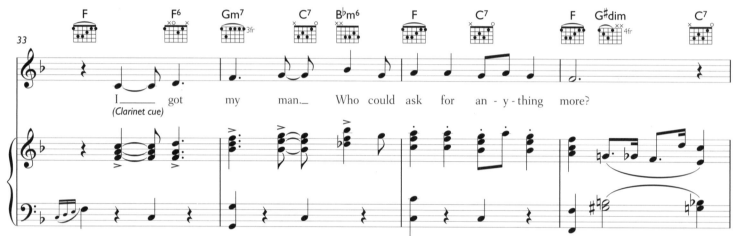

(Clarinet cue) I_____ got my man.___ Who could ask for an - y - thing more?

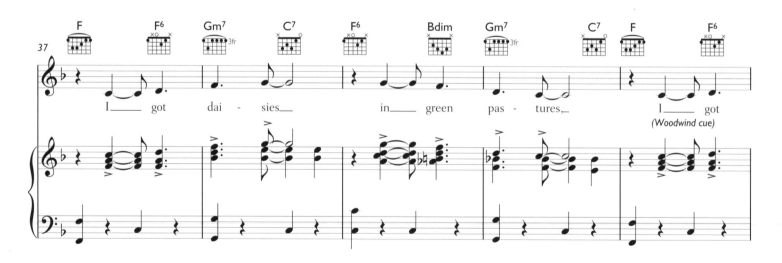

I_____ got dai - sies_____ in___ green pas - tures,___ I_____ got *(Woodwind cue)*

my man.___ Who could ask for an - y - thing more? Old___ Man

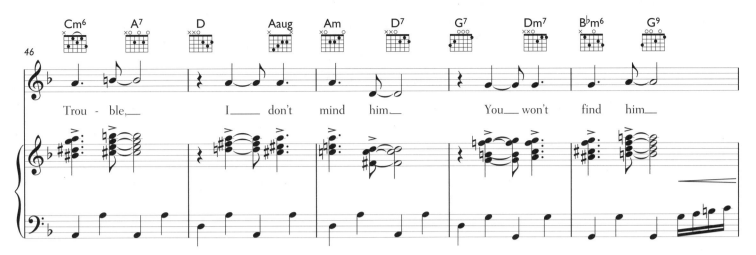

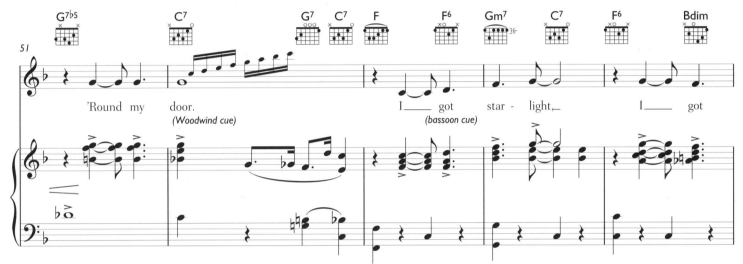

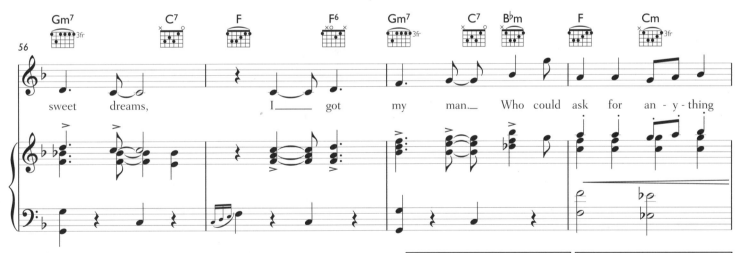

THE MAN THAT GOT AWAY

Words by Ira Gershwin
Music by Harold Arlen

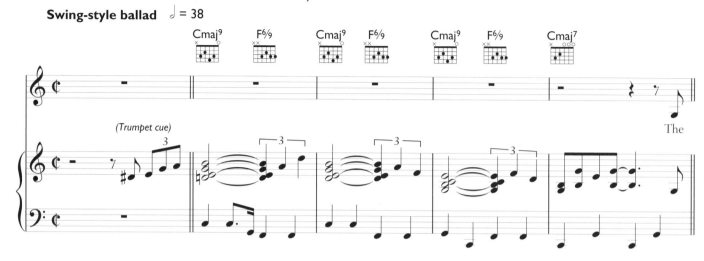

A NIGHTINGALE SANG IN BERKELEY SQUARE

Words by Eric Maschwitz
Music by Manning Sherwin

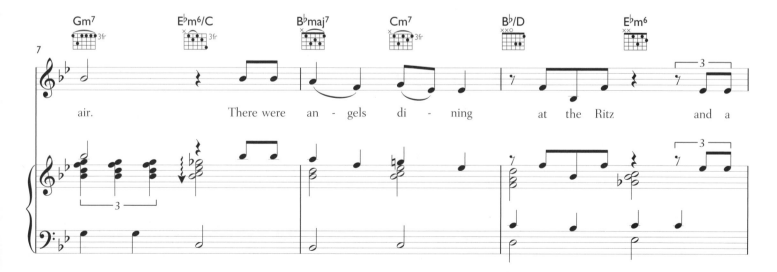

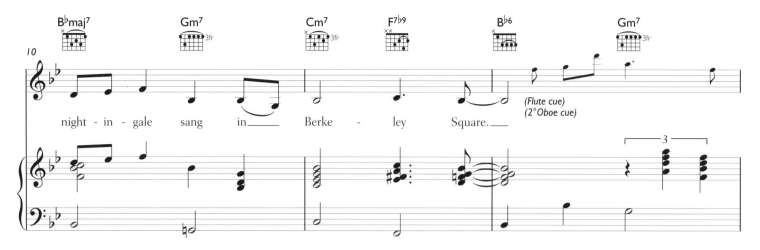

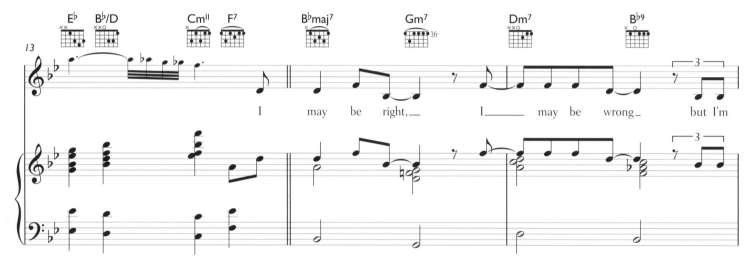

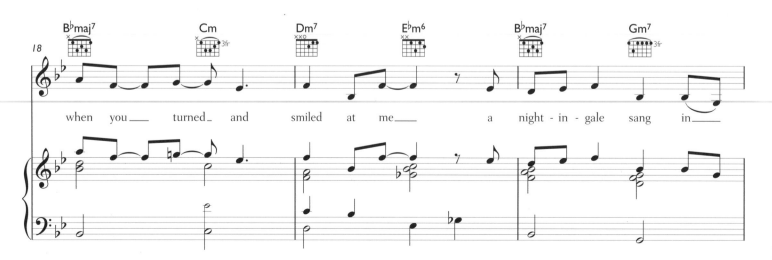

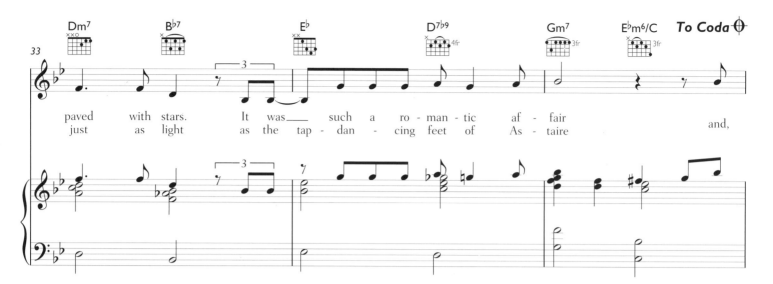

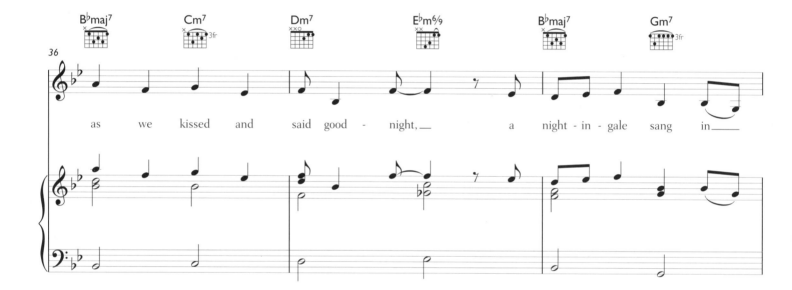

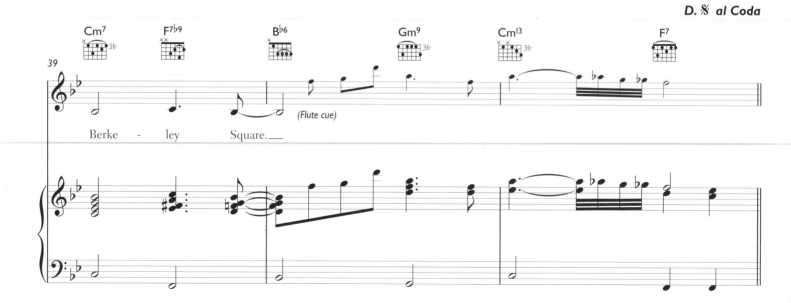

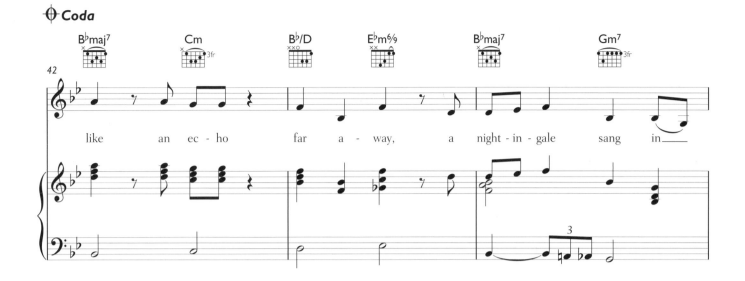

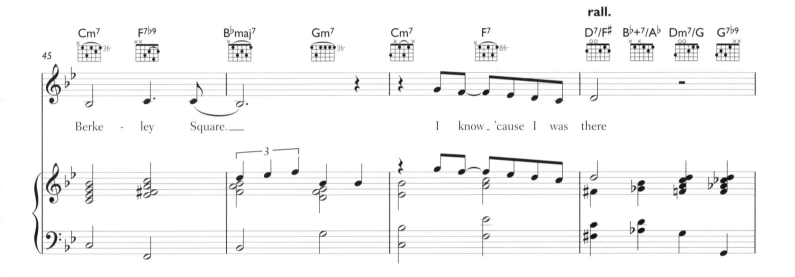

NO MORE TEARS (ENOUGH IS ENOUGH)

Words and Music by Paul Jabara and Bruce Roberts

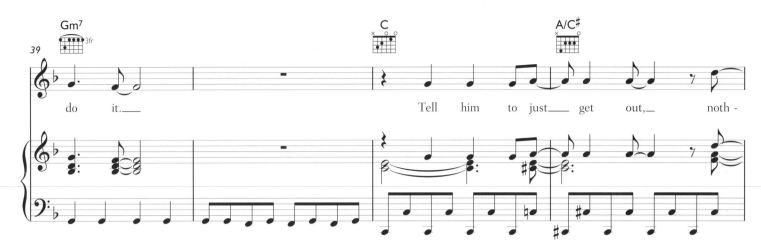

do it.___ Tell him to just___ get out,___ noth-

-ing left to talk___ a-bout.___ Pack his rain-coat, show him out,___ just

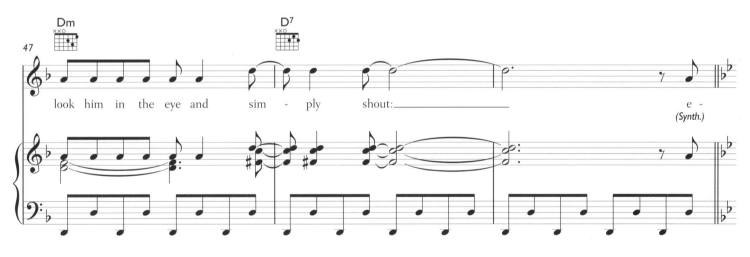

look him in the eye and sim-ply shout:_____ e -
(Synth.)

-nough is e-nough, is e-nough. I can't___ go on, I can't___ go on___

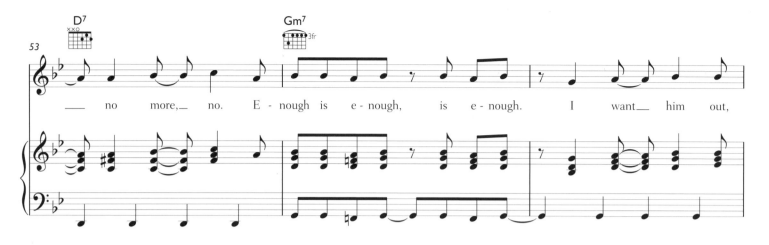

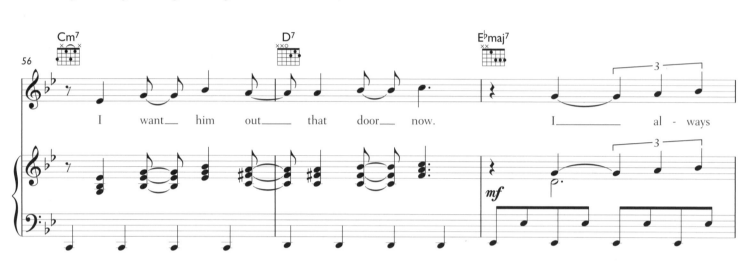

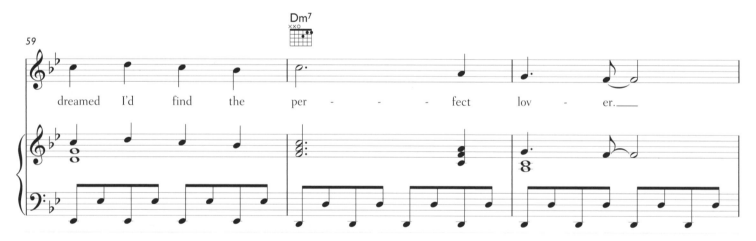

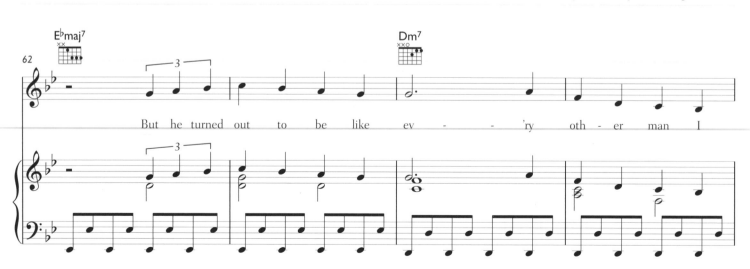

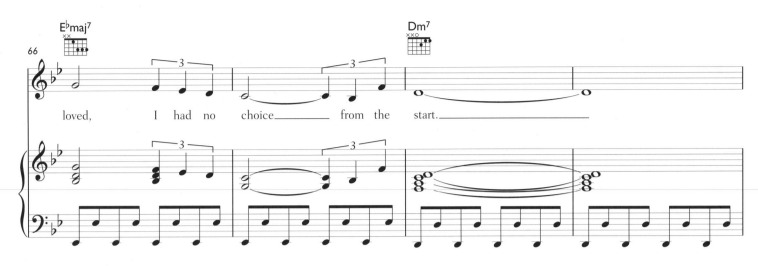

loved, I had no choice_____ from the start._____

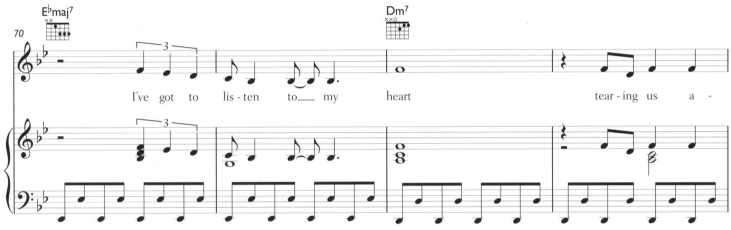

I've got to lis-ten to__ my heart tear-ing us a -

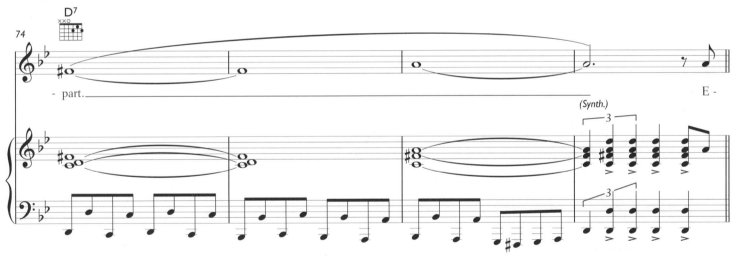

- part._____ E -

-nough is e - nough, is e - nough. I can't__ go on, I can't__ go on__

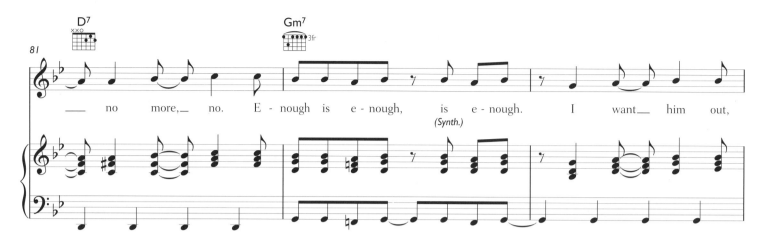

no more, — no. E - nough is e - nough, is e - nough. I want — him out,
(Synth.)

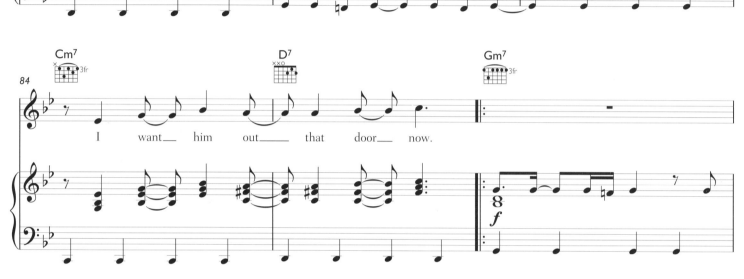

I want — him out — that door — now.

1.

2.

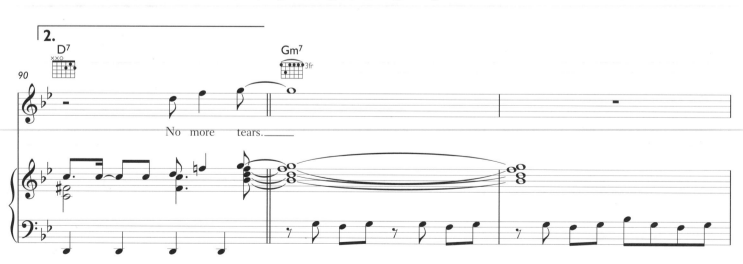

No more tears. —

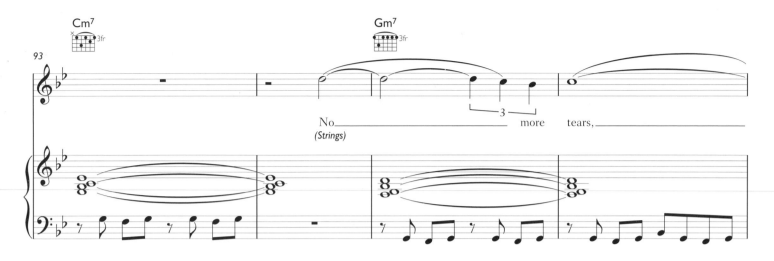

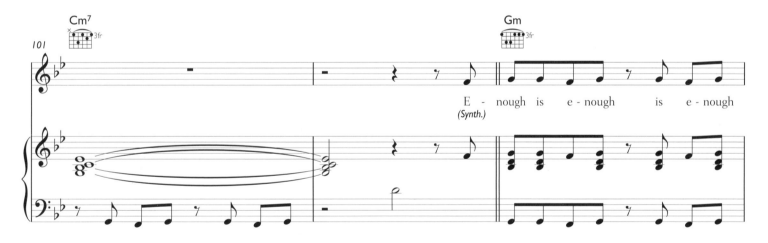

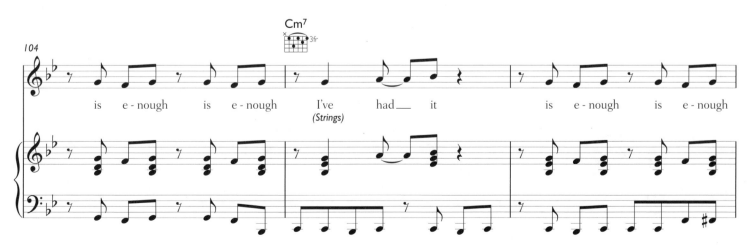

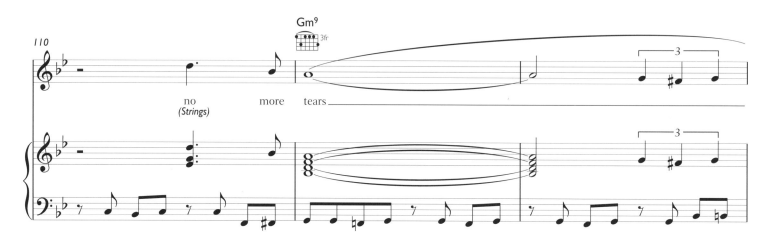

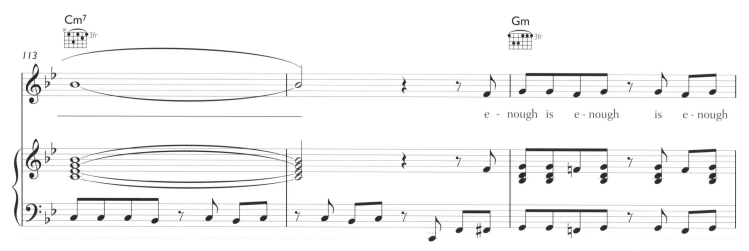

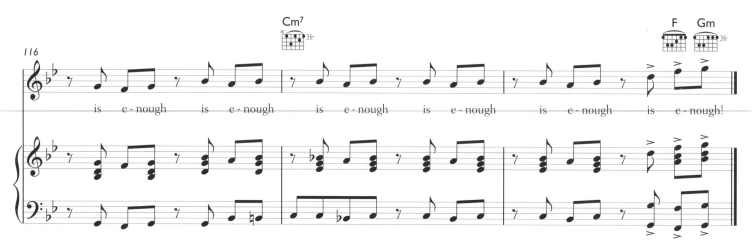

PEOPLE

Words by Bob Merrill
Music by Jule Styne

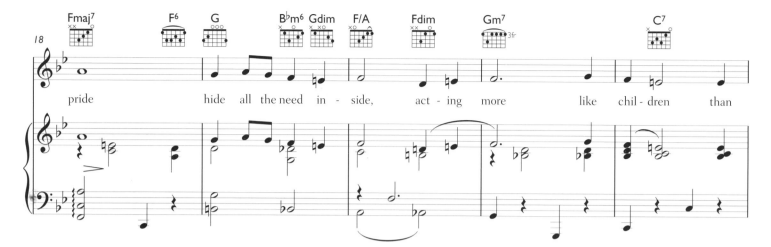

pride   hide all the need in - side,   act - ing more   like chil - dren than

chil - dren._____   Lov - ers_____   are ver - y spe - cial

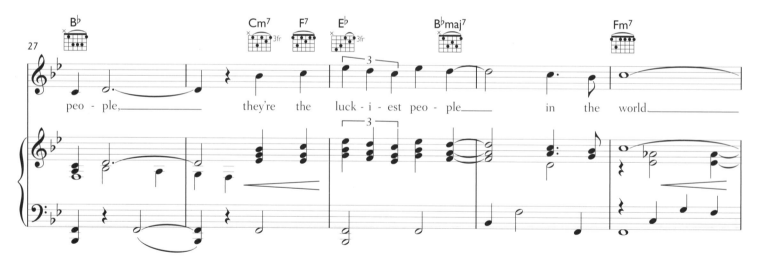

peo - ple,_____   they're the luck - i - est peo - ple_____ in the world_____

___ With one per - son,_____ one ver - y spe - cial per - son,_____ a feel - ing

deep in your soul _____ says: you were half, now you're whole._____ No more

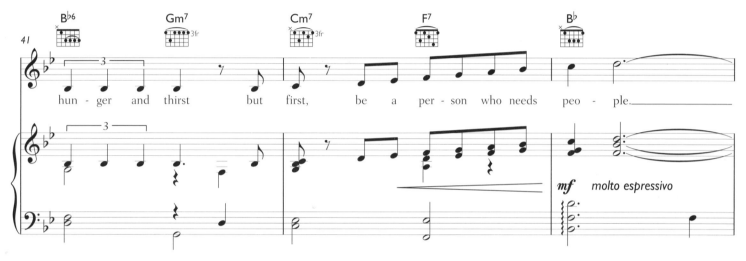

hun - ger and thirst but first, be a per - son who needs peo - ple._____

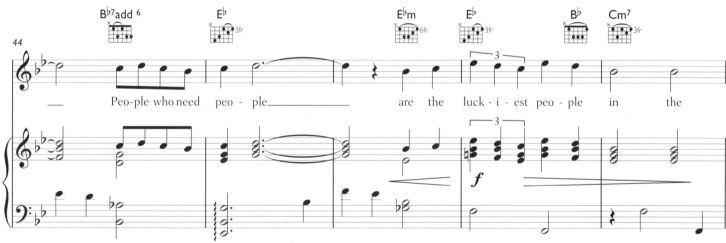

Peo-ple who need peo - ple_____ are the luck - i - est peo-ple in the

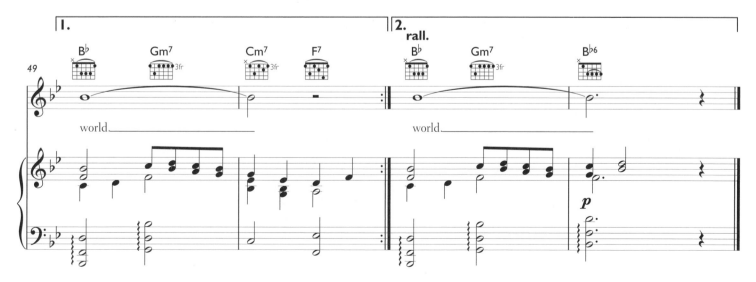

world_____

world_____

SO FAR AWAY

Words and Music by Carole King

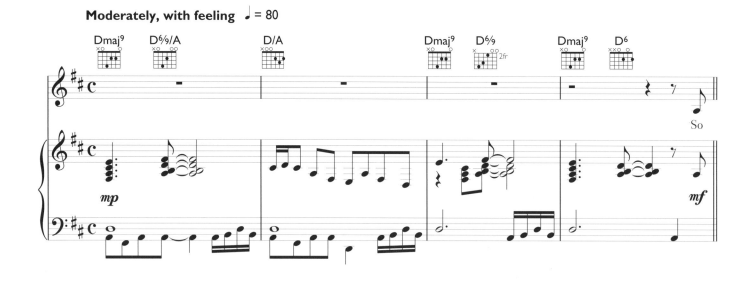

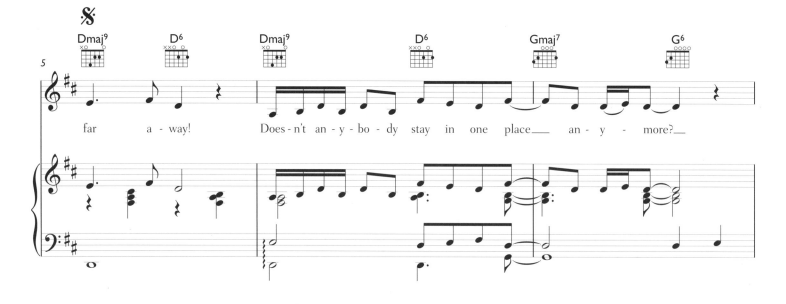

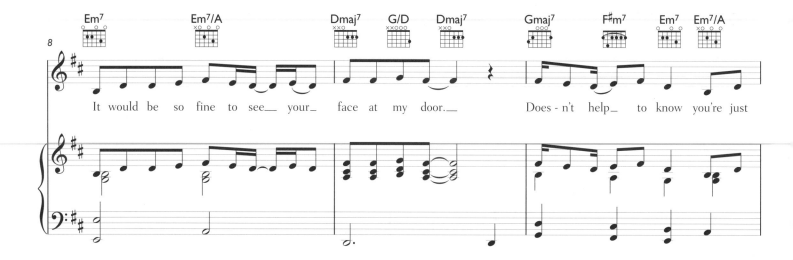

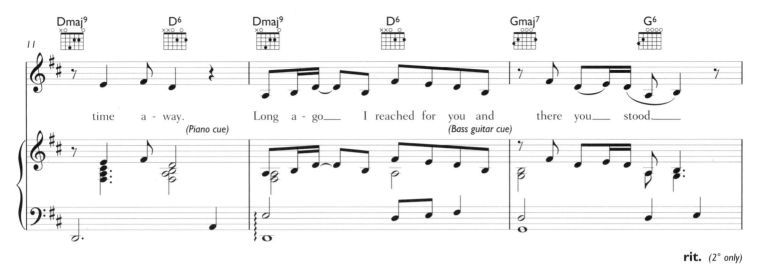

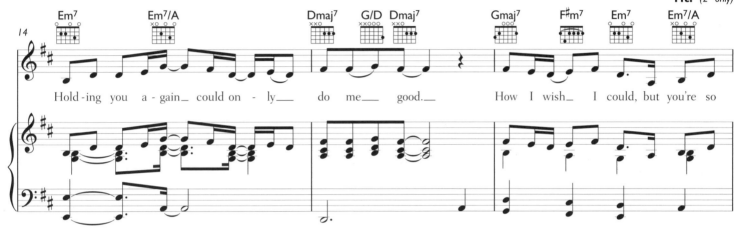

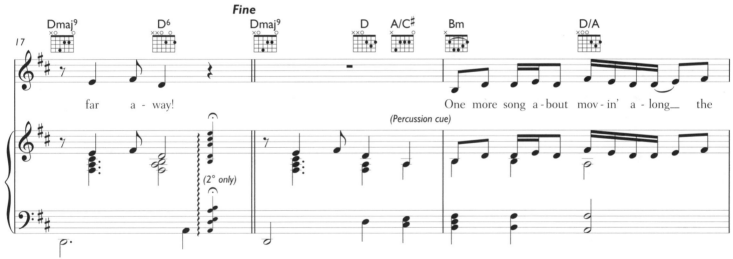

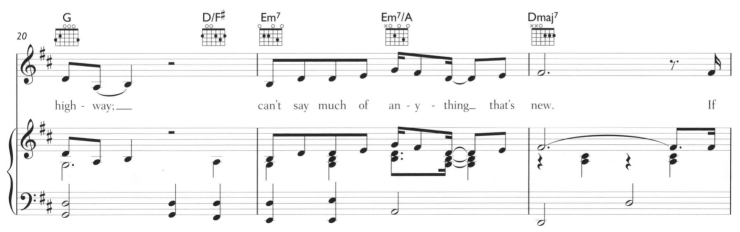

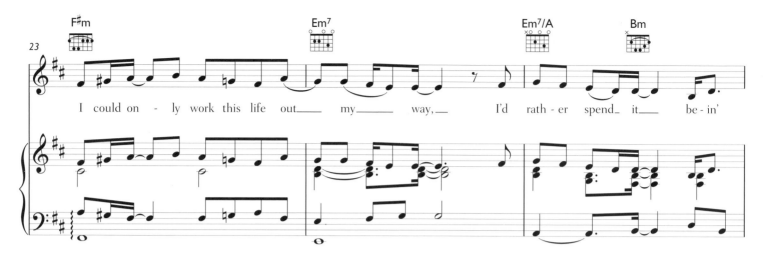

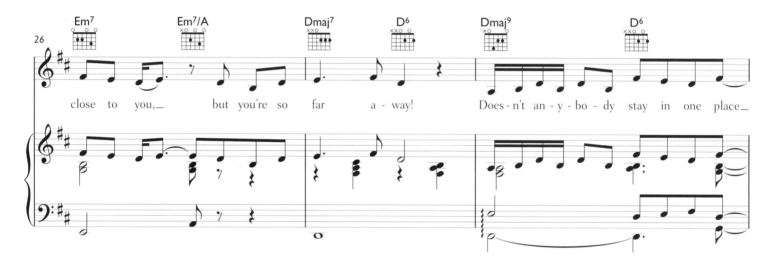

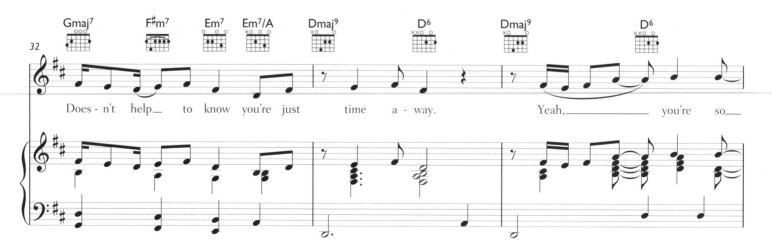

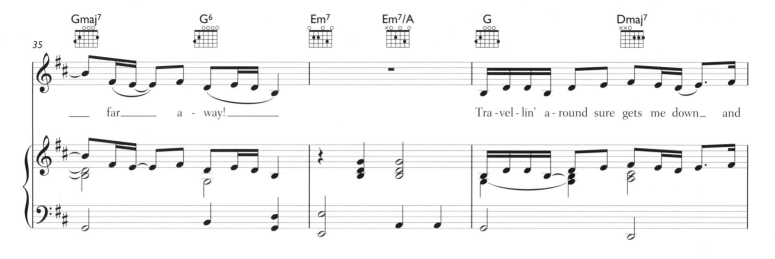

far_____ a - way!_____ Tra - vel - lin' a - round sure gets me down___ and

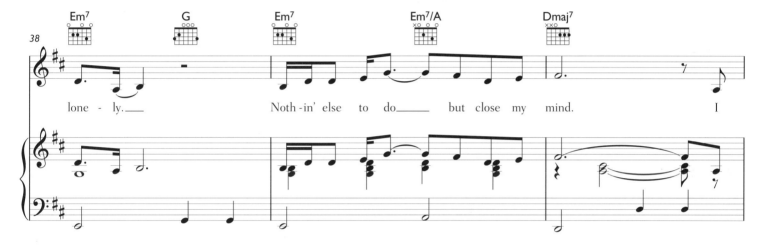

lone - ly.____ Noth - in' else to do____ but close my mind. I

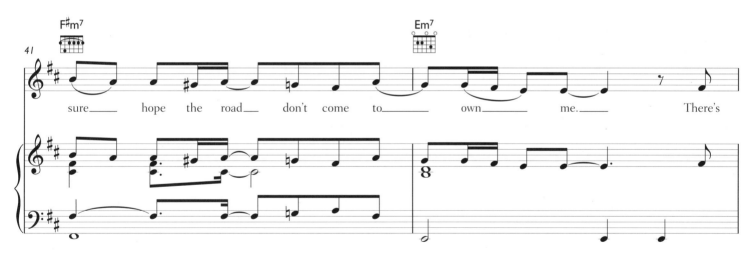

sure____ hope the road____ don't come to____ own____ me.____ There's

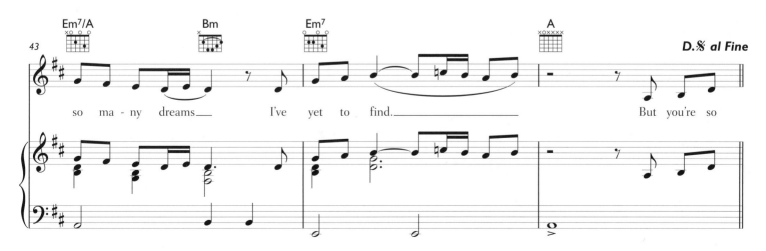

so ma - ny dreams____ I've yet to find._____ But you're so

D.𝄋 al Fine

THERE'S NO BUSINESS LIKE SHOW BUSINESS

Words and Music by Irving Berlin

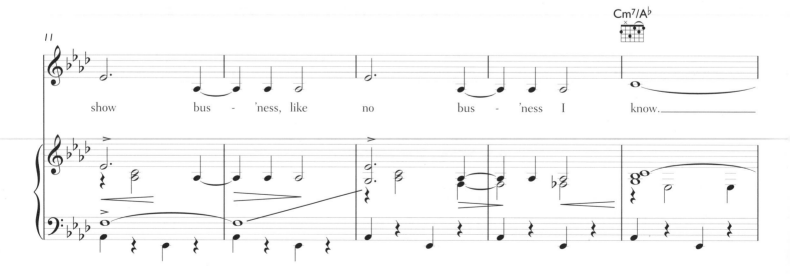

62

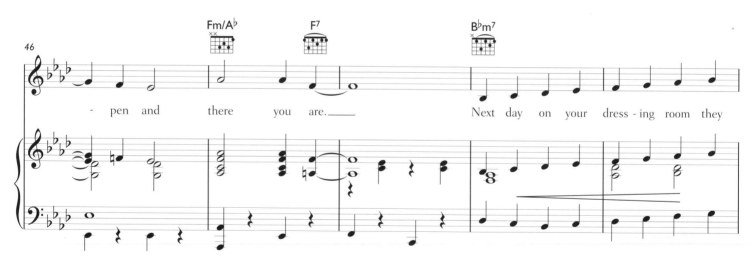

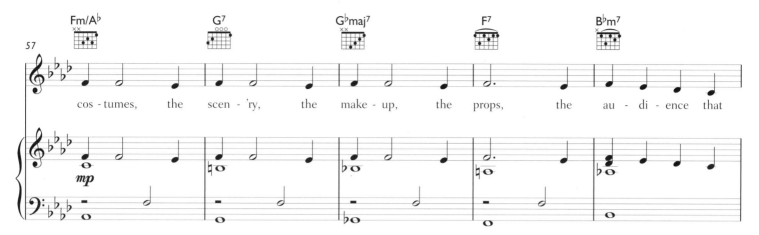

cos - tumes, the scen - 'ry, the make - up, the props, the au - di - ence that

lifts you when you're down._____ The head - aches, the heart - aches, the

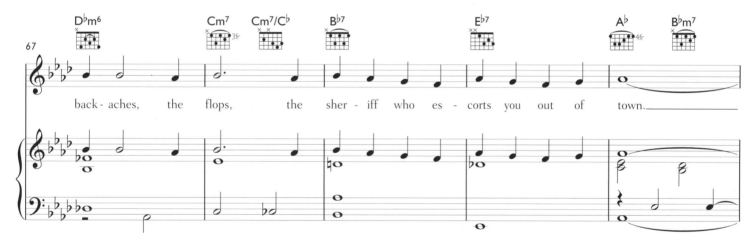

back - aches, the flops, the sher - iff who es - corts you out of town._____

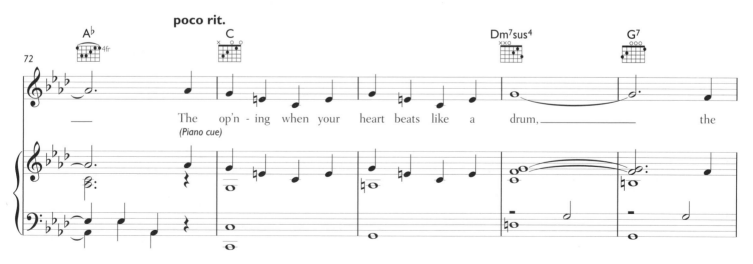

poco rit.

_____ The op'n - ing when your heart beats like a drum,_____ the

(Piano cue)

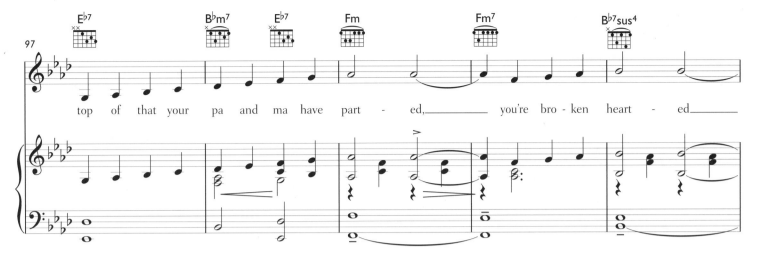

top of that your pa and ma have part - ed,_____ you're bro - ken heart - ed_____

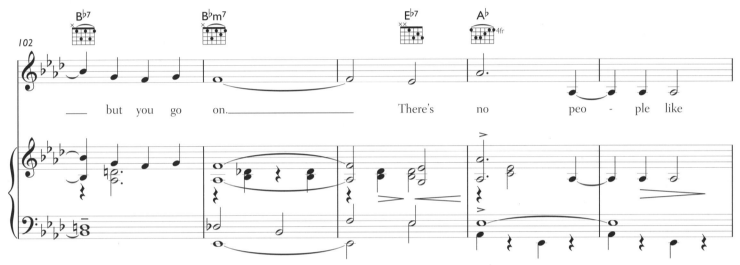

_____ but you go on._____ There's no peo - ple like

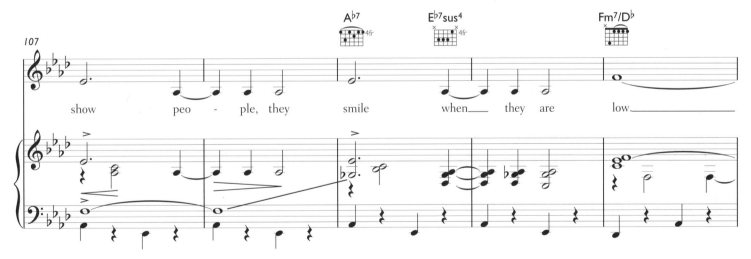

show peo - ple, they smile when____ they are low._____

Ev - en with a tur - key that you know will fold,____ you

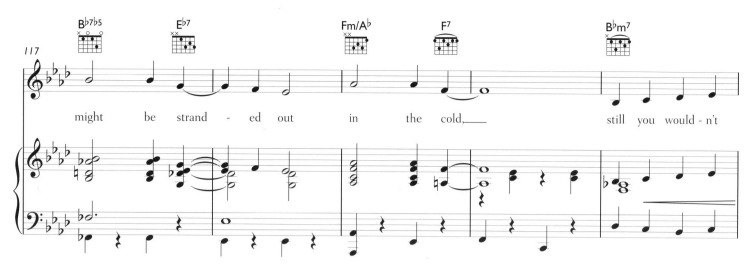

might be strand - ed out in the cold,___ still you would - n't

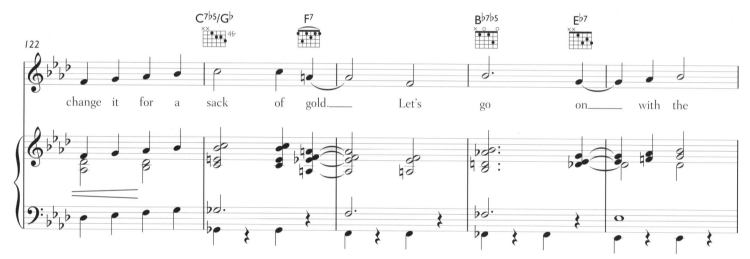

change it for a sack of gold.___ Let's go on___ with the

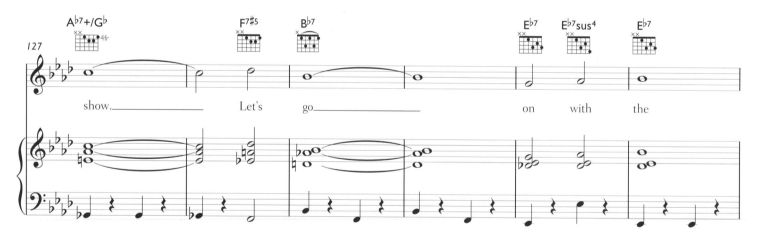

show.___ Let's go___ on with the

poco rit.

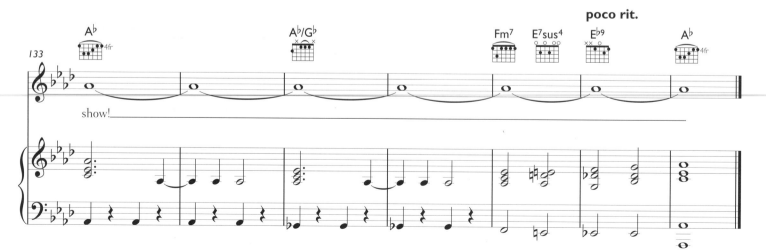

show!___

WHAT A DIFFERENCE A DAY MADE

Words by Stanley Adams
Music by Maria Grever

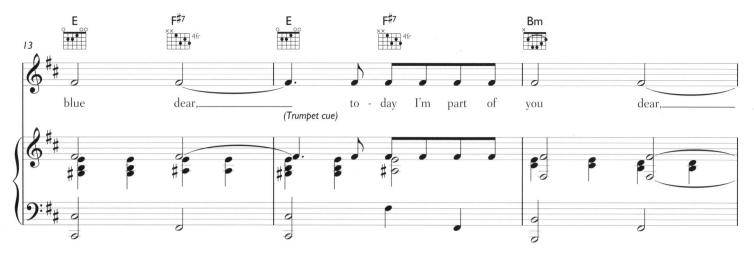

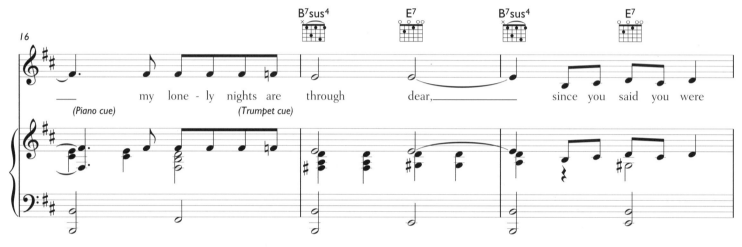

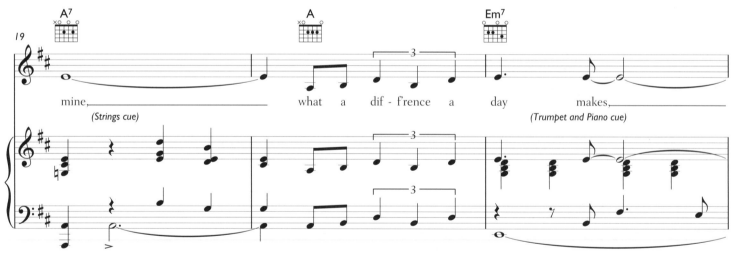

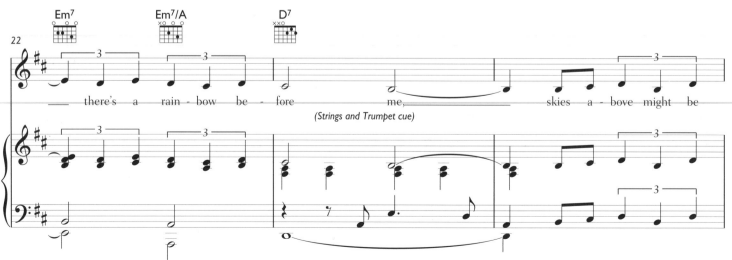

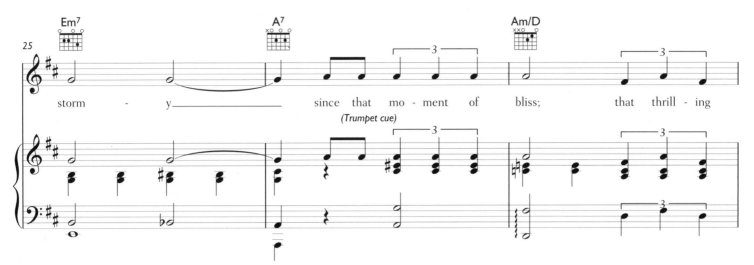

storm - y_____ since that mo - ment of bliss; that thrill - ing
(Trumpet cue)

kiss. It's hea - ven when you,_____ find ro - mance on the
(Trumpet cue)

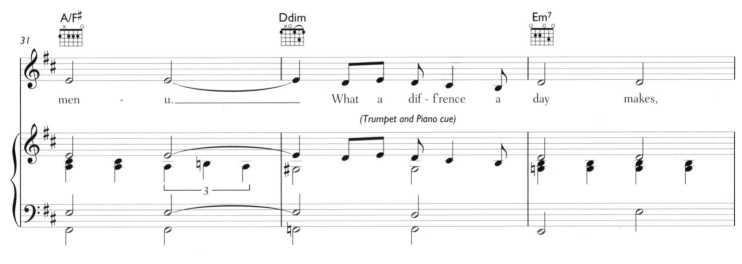

men - u._____ What a dif - frence a day makes,
(Trumpet and Piano cue)

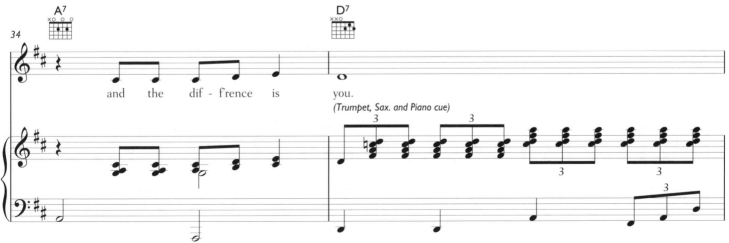

and the dif - frence is you.
(Trumpet, Sax. and Piano cue)

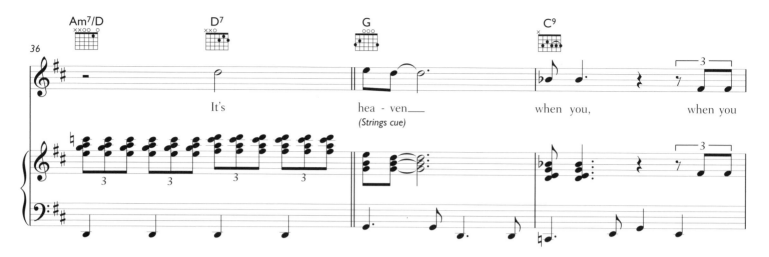

all woman

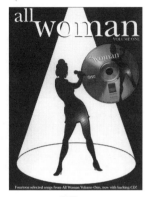

All Woman
VOLUME 1 PVG/CD 7077A

All Woman - Cabaret - Can't Stay Away
From You - Eternal Flame - Ev'ry Time We
Say Goodbye - Get Here - I Am What I Am
I Only Want To Be With You - Miss You
Like Crazy - Nobody Does It Better
The Rose - Summertime - Superwoman
What's Love Got To Do With It

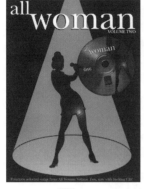

All Woman
VOLUME 2 PVG/CD 7268A

Anytime You Need A Friend
Don't It Make My Brown Eyes Blue
Flashdance....What A Feeling - I'll Stand
By You - Killing Me Softly With His Song
One Moment In Time - Pearl's A Singer
(They Long To Be) Close To You - Think
True Blue - Walk On By - The Wind
Beneath My Wings - You Don't Have To
Say You Love Me - 1-2-3

All Woman
VOLUME 3 PVG/CD 9187A

Almaz - Big Spender - Crazy For You
Fame - From A Distance - My Baby Just
Cares For Me - My Funny Valentine
The Power Of Love - Promise Me
Respect - Take My Breath Away
Total Eclipse Of The Heart

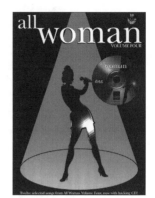

All Woman
VOLUME 4 PVG/CD 9255A

Baby Love - Diamonds Are Forever
Evergreen - For Your Eyes Only - I Will
Survive - If I Could Turn Back Time - I'll
Be There - Rainy Night In Georgia - Send
In The Clowns - Smooth Operator - Sweet
Love - Touch Me In The Morning

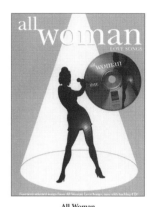

All Woman
LOVE SONGS PVG/CD 7502A

All At Once – Anything For You – Because
You Loved Me – Crazy For You – Didn't We
Almost Have It All – The Greatest Love Of
All – Here We Are – Hero – How Do I Live
I'll Never Love This Way Again – Saving
All My Love For You – Think Twice – The
Wind Beneath My Wings – Without You

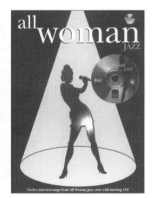

All Woman
JAZZ PVG/CD 9500A

Bewitched – Dream A Little Dream Of Me
A Foggy Day – The Girl From Ipanema
I'm In The Mood For Love – In The
Mood – It Don't Mean A Thing (If It Ain't
Got That Swing) - Misty – Nice Work
If You Can Get It – On Green Dolphin
Street – 'Round Midnight
Where Or When

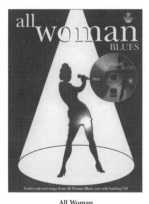

All Woman
BLUES PVG/CD 9550A

The Birth Of The Blues - Come Rain Or
Come Shine - Embraceable You - Georgia
On My Mind - Knock On Wood Mood
Indigo - Night And Day - Rescue Me
Someone To Watch Over Me – Stormy
Weather – Take Another Little Piece Of
My Heart - What Is This Thing
Called Love

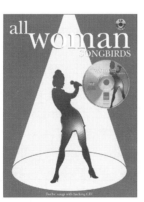

All Woman
Songbirds PVG/CD 9914A

Black Velvet - Can't Fight The Moonlight
Come Away With Me - Fallin' - Feelin'
The Same Way - Over The Rainbow
People Get Ready - The Power Of Love
Substitute For Love - Thank You - There
You'll Be - You Were Meant For Me

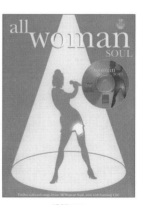

All Woman
SOUL PVG/CD 9668A

Car Wash – Chain Of Fools – Dancing In
The Street - I Put A Spell On You – Jimmy
Mack – Lady Marmalade – Reach Out, I'll
Be There – Stop! In The Name Of Love
Woman – You Can't Hurry Love – You're
All I Need To Get By – Your Love Is King

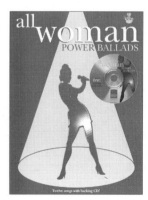

All Woman
Power Ballads PVG/CD 10008A

I Try - I Turn To You - I'm Not A Girl, Not
Yet A Woman - It Must Have Been Love
Lost Without You - Love Don't Cost A
Thing - My Heart Will Go On - The Power
Of Love - Say What You Want - What A
Wonderful World - White Flag - You Don't
Know My Name

Available from all good music shops

AW3

YOU'RE THE VOICE

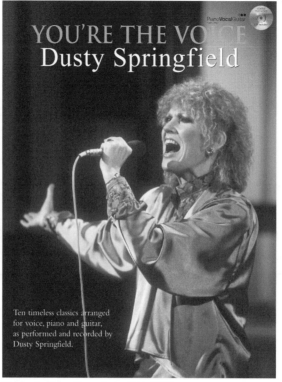

You're the Voice: Dusty Springfield (PVG)
ISBN: 0-571-52502-4
EAN13: 978-0-571-52502-7

All I See Is You
Goin' Back
I Close My Eyes And Count To Ten
I Just Don't Know What To Do With Myself
I Only Want To Be With You
The Look Of Love
Losing You
Some Of Your Lovin'
Son Of A Preacher Man
You Don't Have To Say You Love Me

The outstanding vocal series from Faber Music
CD contains full backings for each song,
professionally arranged to recreate the sounds of the original recording

FABER ff MUSIC